AF413635

The Loyalists and the Patriots: The Revolutionary War Factions

History Picture Books | Children's History Books

In this book, we're going to talk about the Loyalists and the Patriots during the American Revolutionary War. So, let's get right to it!

FREEDOM

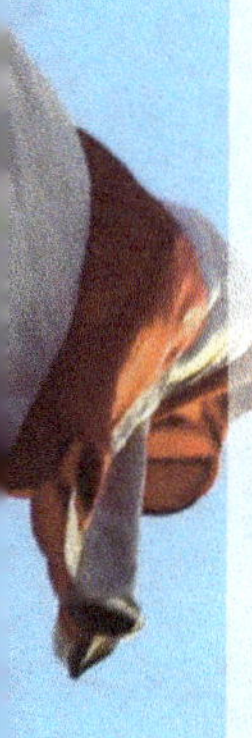

When the pilgrims and other settlers came to America, one of the important reasons was that they wanted to have freedom. They wanted freedom to live as they wanted and freedom to worship as they wanted. The people who founded the thirteen colonies in America were very adventurous.

They knew the dangers they would face as they traveled from Europe to settle in a new country. There were no buildings or farms when they came in 1620. At the beginning, the Native Americans were friendly, until they realized that the settlers were taking over their land.

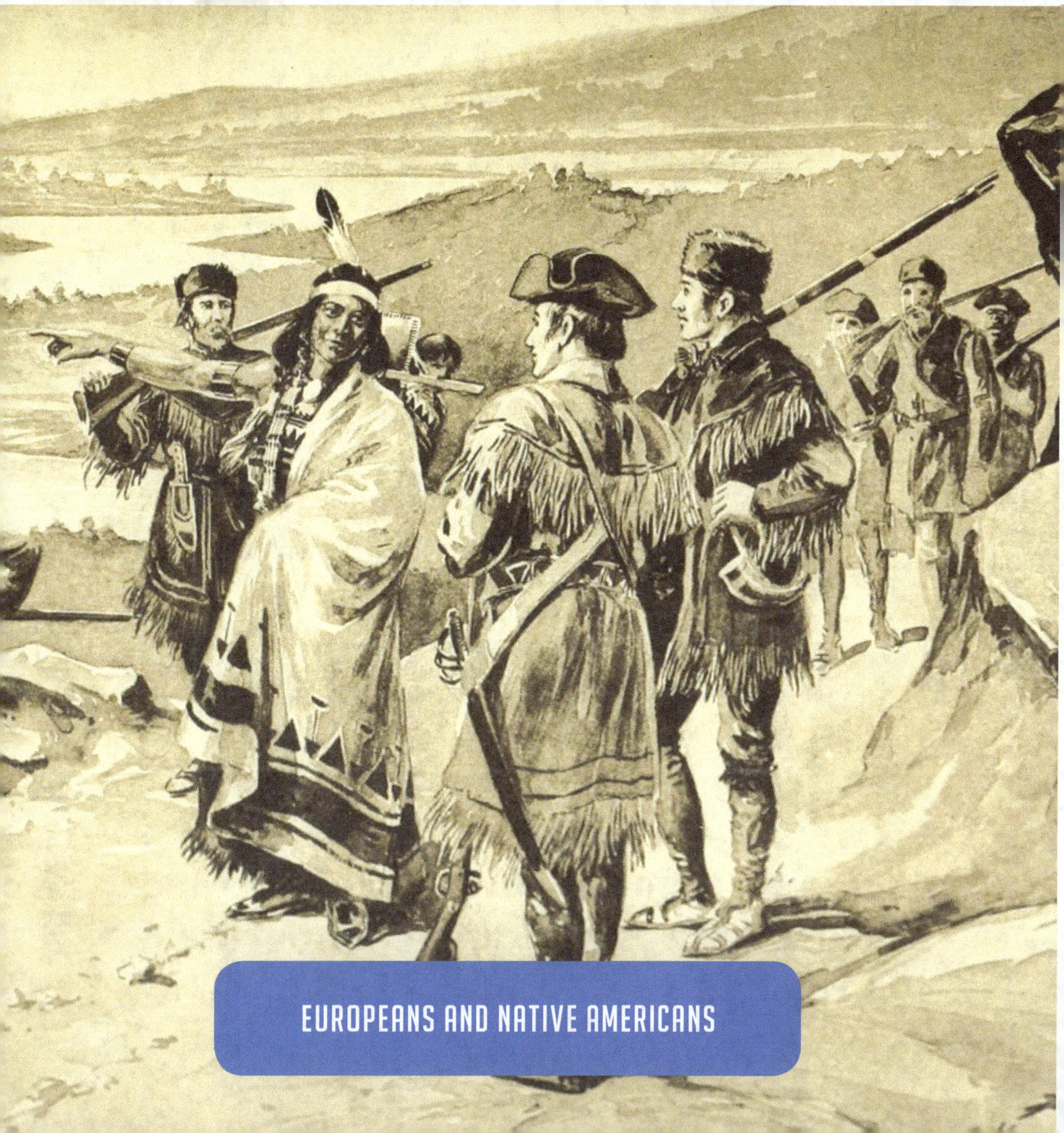

EUROPEANS AND NATIVE AMERICANS

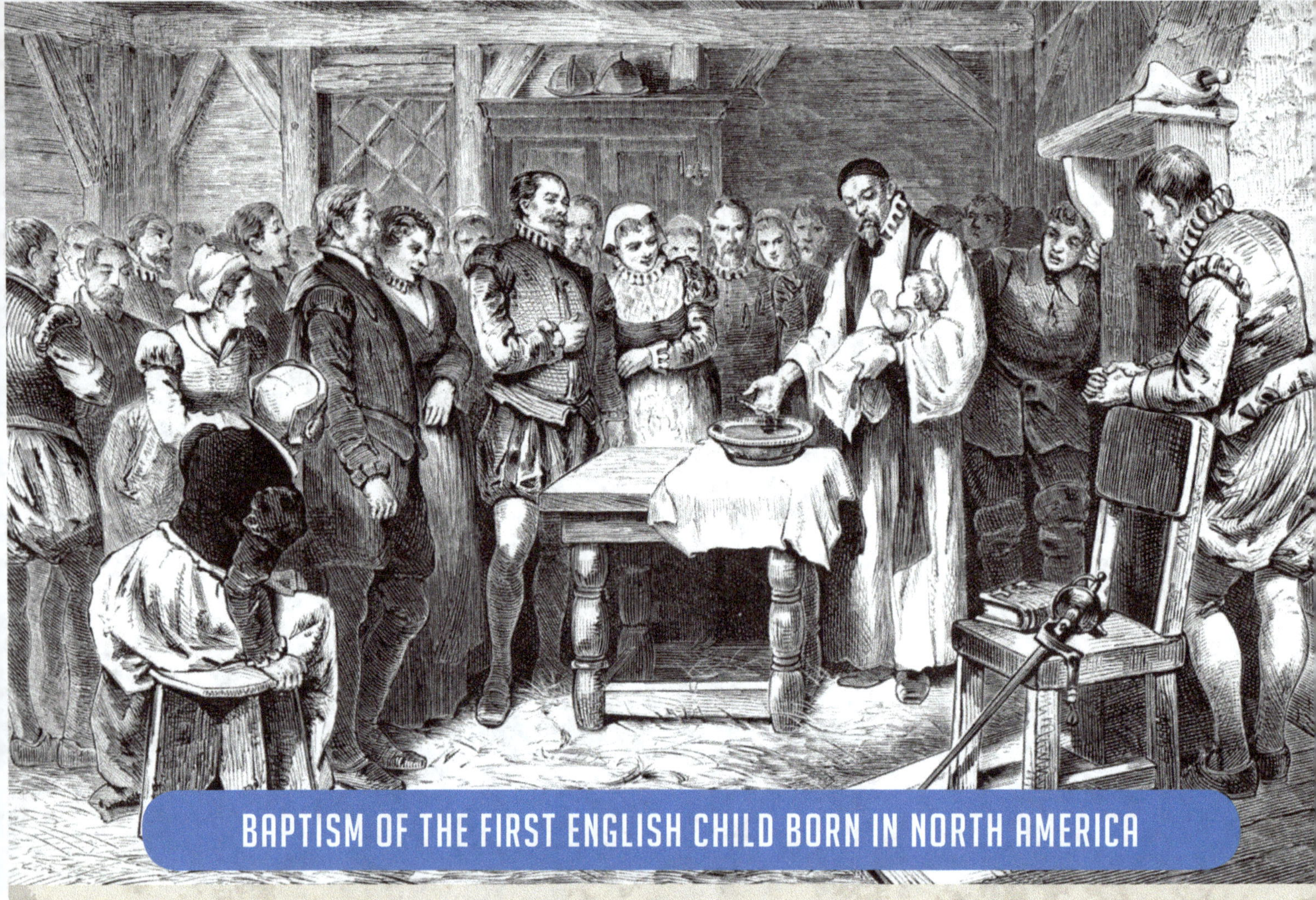

The colonies the settlers had founded were under British rule, but they were far away from the parent country. Living in America was very different from living in England.

For the most part, they set up their own local governments and the British rulers didn't interfere very much. This was true for over 150 years and the colonists got used to having a lot of independence. However, all that changed after the Seven Years' War.

BRITISH AND FRENCH WAR

THE SEVEN YEARS' WAR

The British and the French were often at war with each other throughout the centuries. In the early 1750s, the British were at war with the French in Europe. Eventually, the war spread to North America as well, where both countries owned land.

The war on the North American continent was called the French and Indian War, which lasted from 1754-1763. The war started when the French tried to push the British out of the Ohio River valley. The British declared war. During this time, the colonists were under British rule, so they fought with the British against France. Different Native American tribes fought on each side.

FRENCH AND INDIAN WAR

FRENCH REVOLUTIONARY WAR

The British won the French and Indian War. However, the war, both in Europe and in North America, had been very expensive. The British needed money so they started to heavily tax the colonists. They began to issue a series of Acts that were all designed to tax the thirteen colonies and cut down on the freedoms that the citizens had.

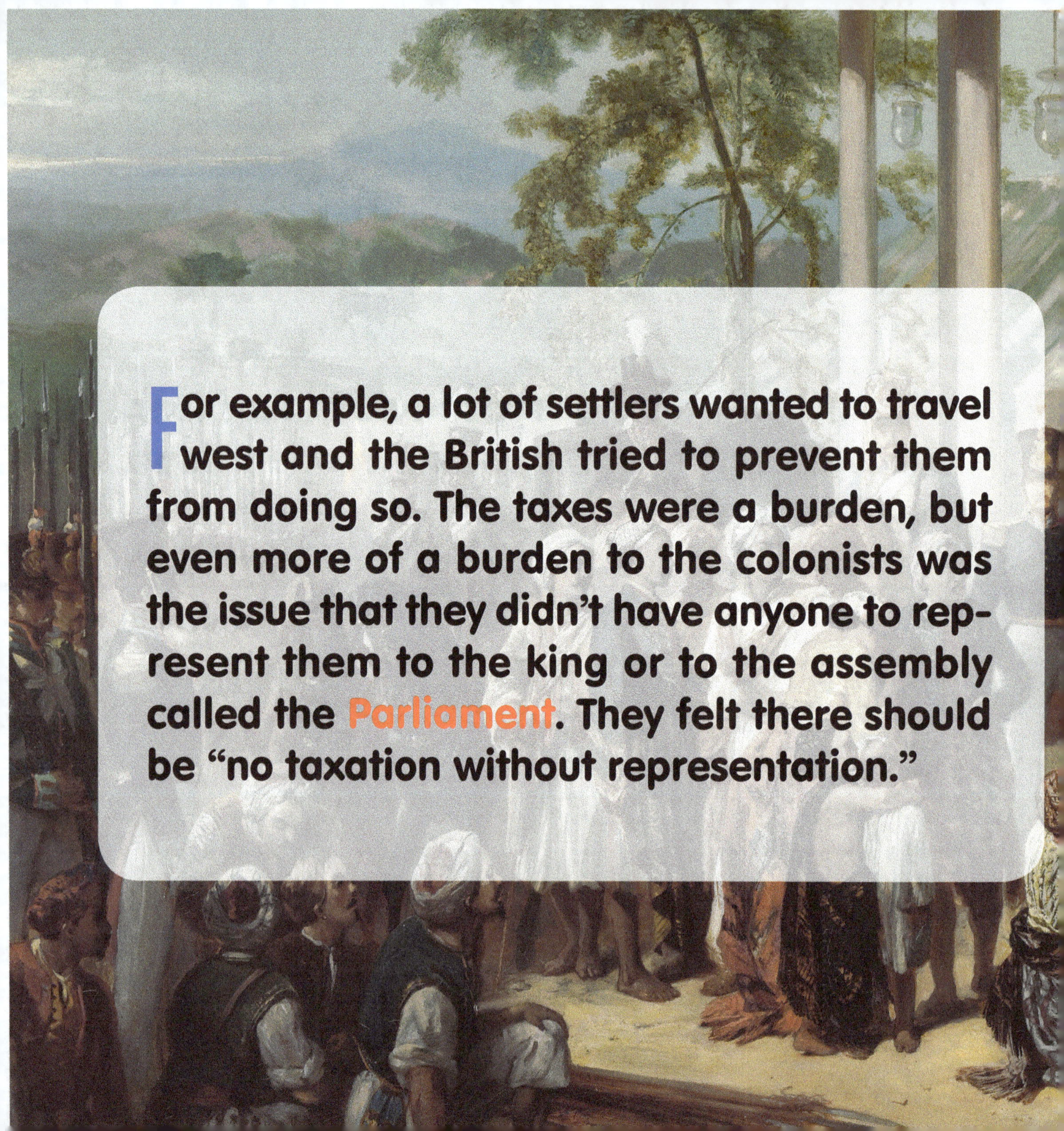
For example, a lot of settlers wanted to travel west and the British tried to prevent them from doing so. The taxes were a burden, but even more of a burden to the colonists was the issue that they didn't have anyone to represent them to the king or to the assembly called the Parliament. They felt there should be "no taxation without representation."

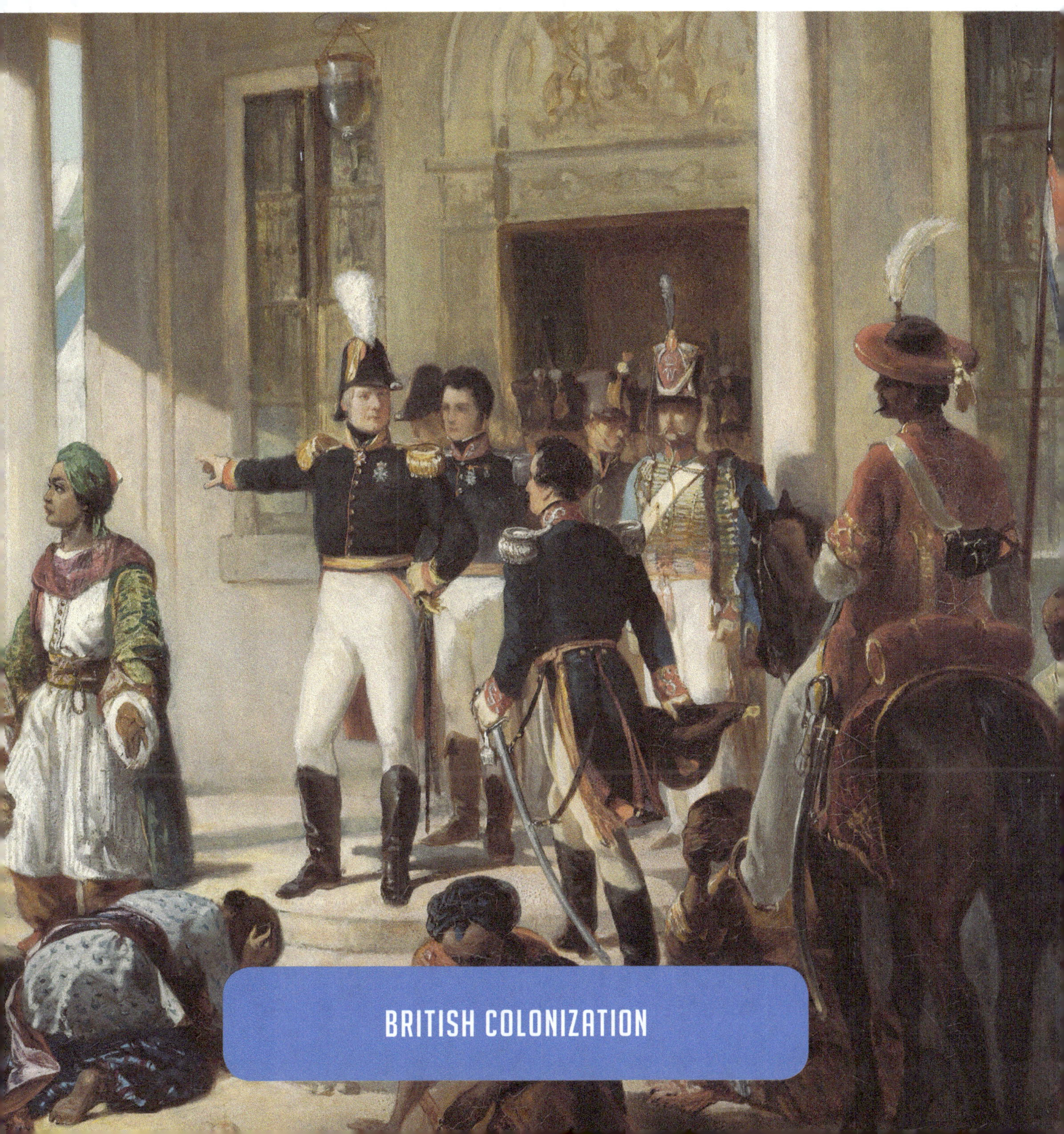

BRITISH COLONIZATION

GOVERNOR BERKELEY BARING HIS BREAST FOR BACON
TO SHOOT AFTER REFUSING HIM A COMMISSION

As the British continued to levy more and more taxes on the colonists, the growing unrest led the citizens of the colonies to declare their intentions either for or against Britain.

WHO BECAME PATRIOTS?

At the beginning, the colonists claimed that all they wanted was representation in the British government. However, as time went on, a growing number were very clear that they wanted to be completely independent of Britain's rule.

EVACUATION DAY

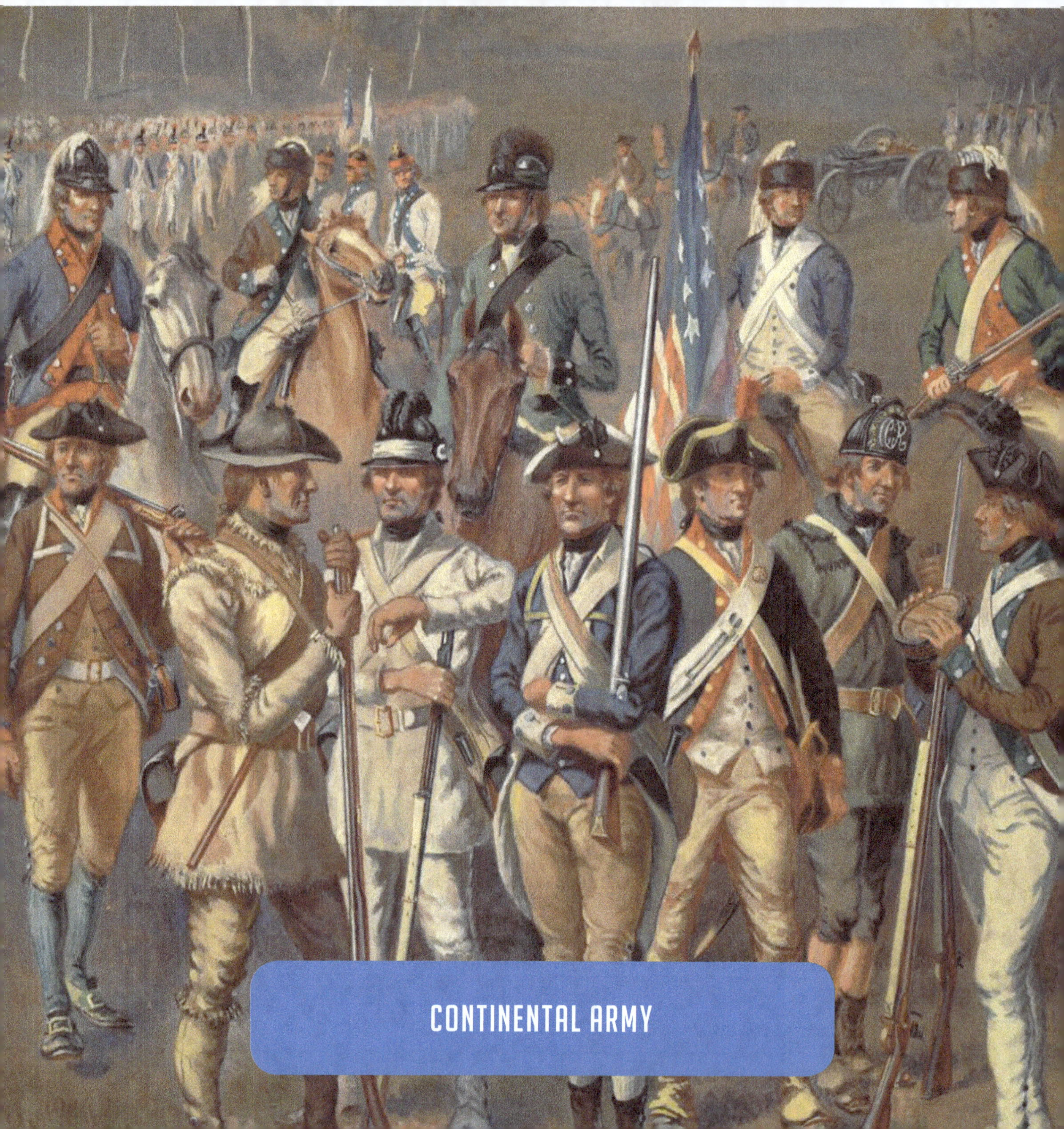

CONTINENTAL ARMY

They wanted their own country where they could keep the freedoms that they had risked so much to gain. The British weren't treating them fairly. They felt that it was time to "break up" with Britain. The Patriots were willing to go up against the British to get what they wanted. They were willing to fight for liberty. About 40-45% of the colonists became Patriots.

FAMOUS PATRIOTS

If the Patriots hadn't been successful in their fight against the British, the world probably wouldn't know any of their names today. They would have been convicted of treason and may have been put to death if they survived the war.

CONTINENTAL ARMY

GEORGE WASHINGTON

However, the Patriots did win and many of these brave men became influential in the government of the new nation, the United States of America. All of these men were famous Patriots:

★ **George Washington,** Commander-in-Chief of the Continental Army during the war and eventually first President of the United States

★ **Benjamin Franklin,** one of the Founding Fathers of the United States

★ **John Adams,** 2nd President of the United States

★ **Thomas Jefferson,** author of the Declaration of Independence and 3rd President of the United States

★ **Paul Revere,** a silversmith and Patriot, he developed a system of using lanterns to warn Minutemen that the British were coming

★ **Patrick Henry,** a famous speaker led the fight against the Stamp Act and who spoke the phrase "Give Me Liberty or Give Me Death."

★ **Samuel Adams,** one of the Founding Fathers

Some of these men became Founding Fathers of the new country.

THE SONS OF LIBERTY

The Sons of Liberty was a secret organization of Patriots led by Samuel Adams. They made strategic plans to defeat the British by undermining their authority starting with the protest of the Stamp Act and the Boston Tea Party.

BRITISH LOYALISM

WHO BECAME LOYALISTS?

Not everyone living in the colonies wanted to break away and become independent. Many people wanted to remain loyal to Britain and to the king. The people who wanted to remain under British rule were called **Loyalists**. About 20-30% of the citizens in the colonies considered themselves to be Loyalists.

WHY DID SOME PEOPLE REMAIN LOYAL?

There were many reasons why some colonists chose to remain loyal to the British. Many felt that their quality of life would be better under British rule. Britain had been around for many centuries. Starting a new country was a risky business. Many of the Loyalists wanted to retain the British tradition and lifestyle.

BRITISH LOYALISTS

18TH CENTURY BRITISH MILITARY PARADE REENACTMENT

Some were afraid to fight the British since at that time they were a major military power. Still others had business ties to England and were concerned about how a war would affect those interests.

FAMOUS LOYALISTS

Some colonists who were very influential in their local governments became Loyalists instead of Patriots. Just as the Patriots were considered traitors by the British and the Loyalists, the Patriots felt these important leaders should be fighting for the new nation.

UNITED EMPIRE LOYALISTS STATUE IN HAMILTON

BENEDICT ARNOLD

For example, Benedict Arnold was considered a traitor since he left his position serving as a Continental Army general and switched sides to fight for the British. All of these men were famous Loyalists:

★ **Benedict Arnold, the name "Benedict Arnold" still means a traitor today**

★ **Joseph Galloway, a delegate to the Continental Congress, he switched sides to fight for the British as a Loyalist**

★ **Thomas Hutchinson, an important**

Loyalist politician and governor of the colony of Massachusetts

★ **Andrew Allen,** a representative for Pennsylvania in the Second Continental Congress but then switched sides to fight for the British

★ **John Butler,** leader of a militia called Butler's Rangers

★ **David Mathews,** mayor of the city of New York

THOMAS HUTCHINSON

YANKEE DOODLE

DID EVERY CITIZEN BECOME A PATRIOT OR LOYALIST?

Many people tried to remain neutral during the war. Somewhere in the range of 25-40% of the citizens in the colonies didn't pick a side, at least not at the beginning of the Revolutionary War.

WHAT HAPPENED TO LOYALISTS DURING THE WAR?

If you were a Loyalist during the war, your life was very dangerous and difficult. Your home or business could be vandalized by Patriots at any time. Some Loyalists traveled back to Britain. Others helped the British fight against the Patriots. The Loyal Greens were a group of Loyalist fighters and so were the Royal American Regiment.

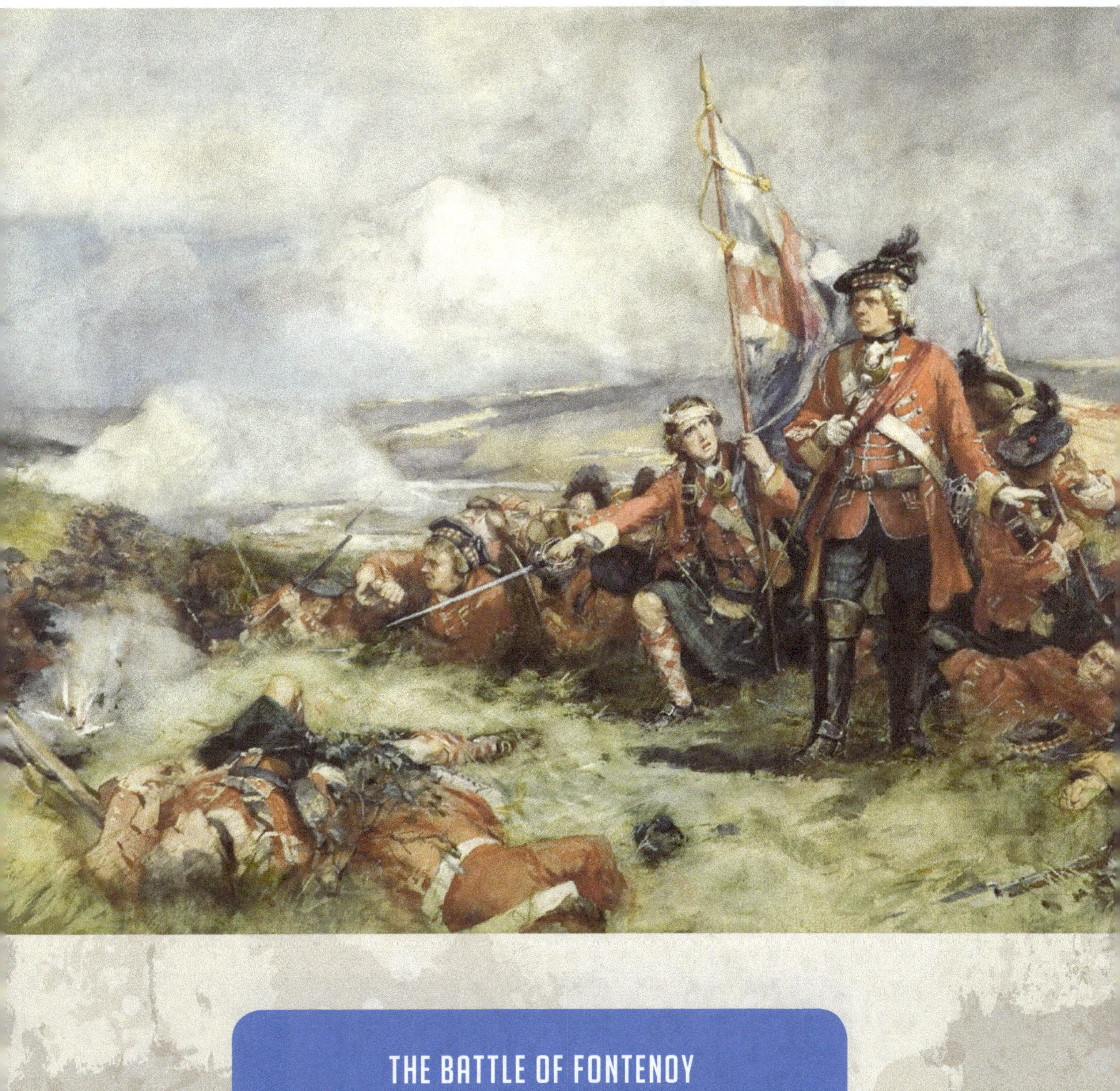

THE BATTLE OF FONTENOY

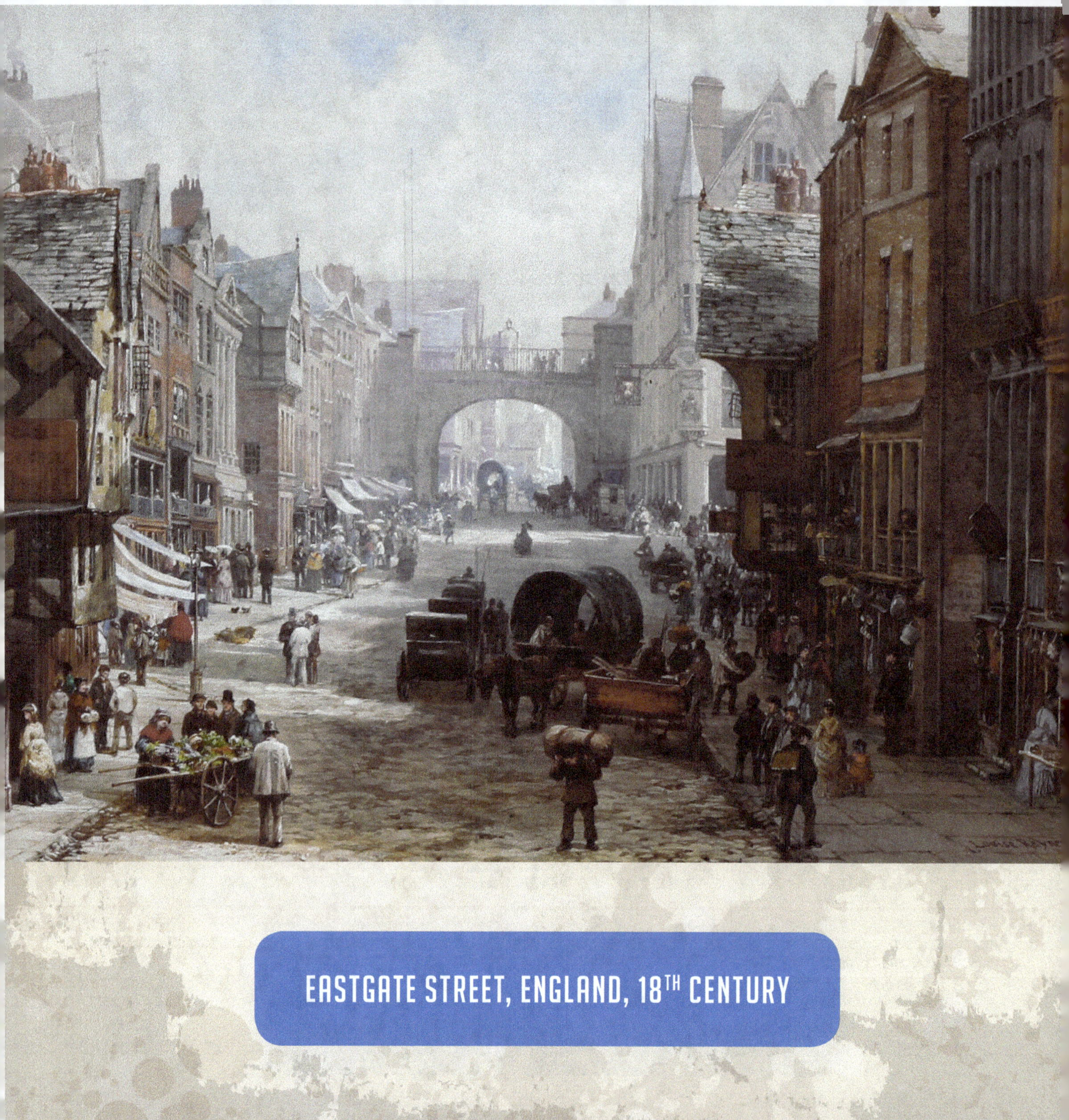

EASTGATE STREET, ENGLAND, 18TH CENTURY

WHAT HAPPENED TO LOYALISTS AFTER THE WAR?

After the war was over, many Loyalists returned to England. If they had property or wealth in the colonies, it was lost to them now and they had to start all over again.

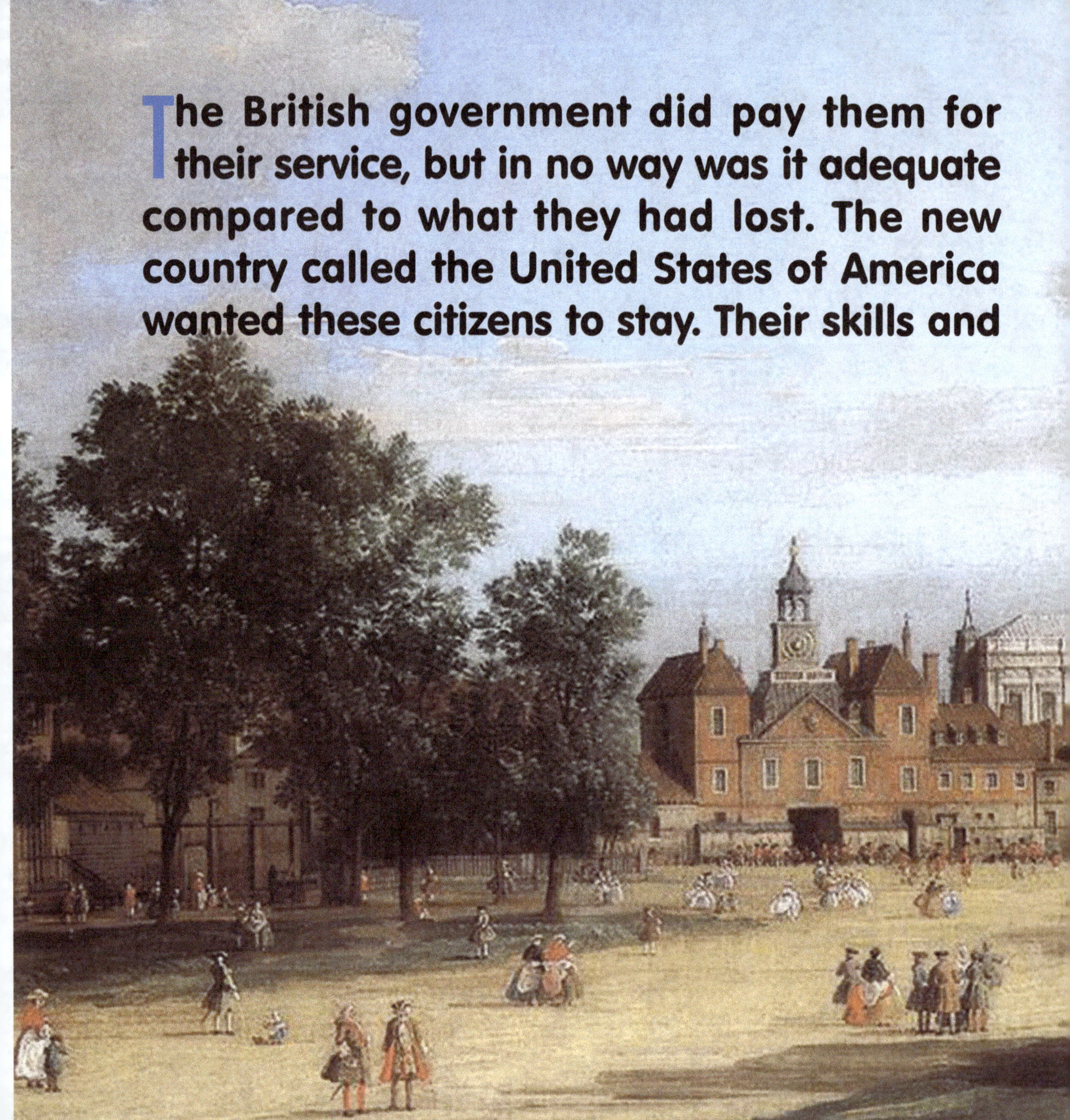
The British government did pay them for their service, but in no way was it adequate compared to what they had lost. The new country called the United States of America wanted these citizens to stay. Their skills and

educational experience would have been helpful in building the economy in the new country. Despite this, very few Loyalists decided to stay.

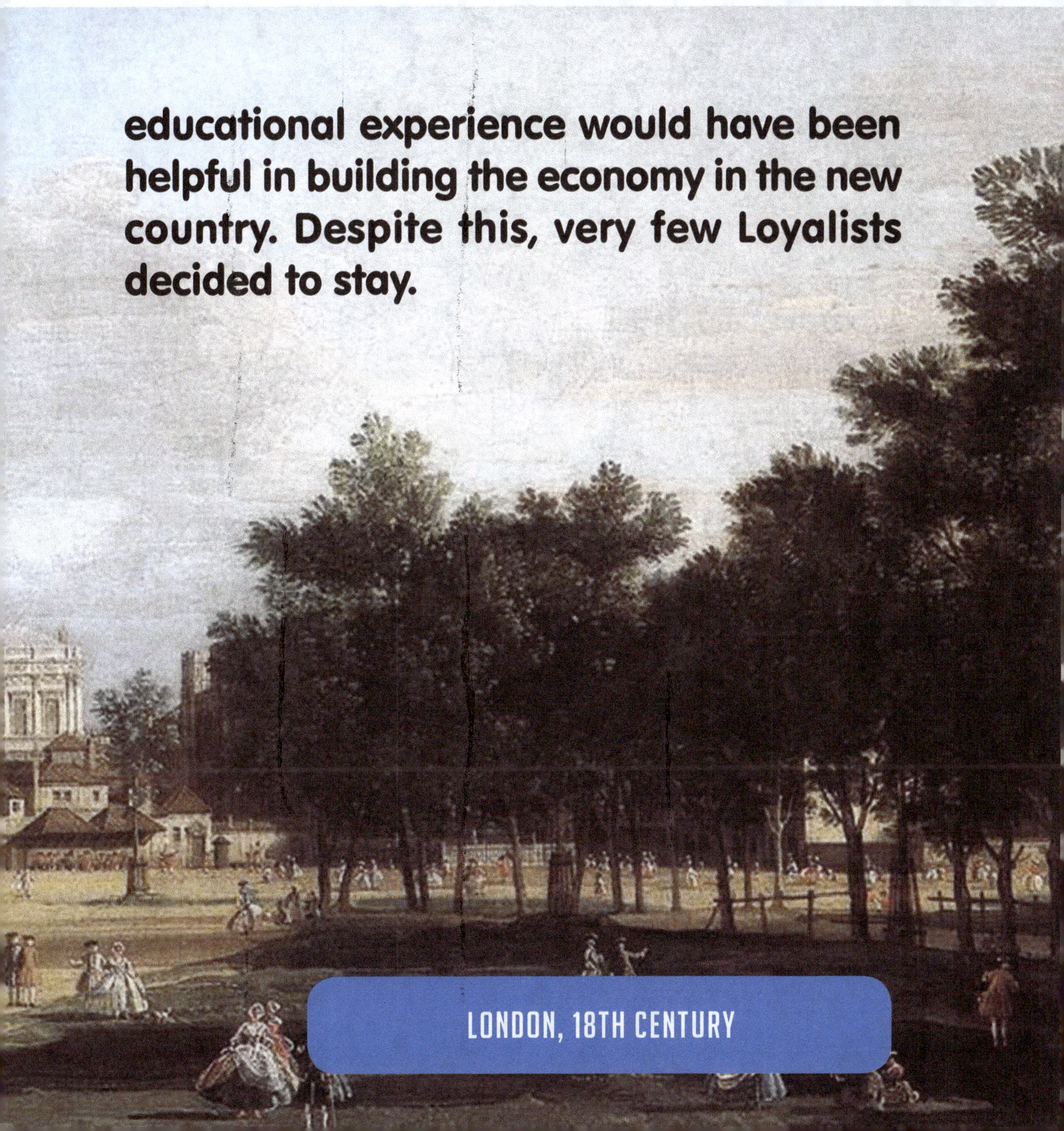

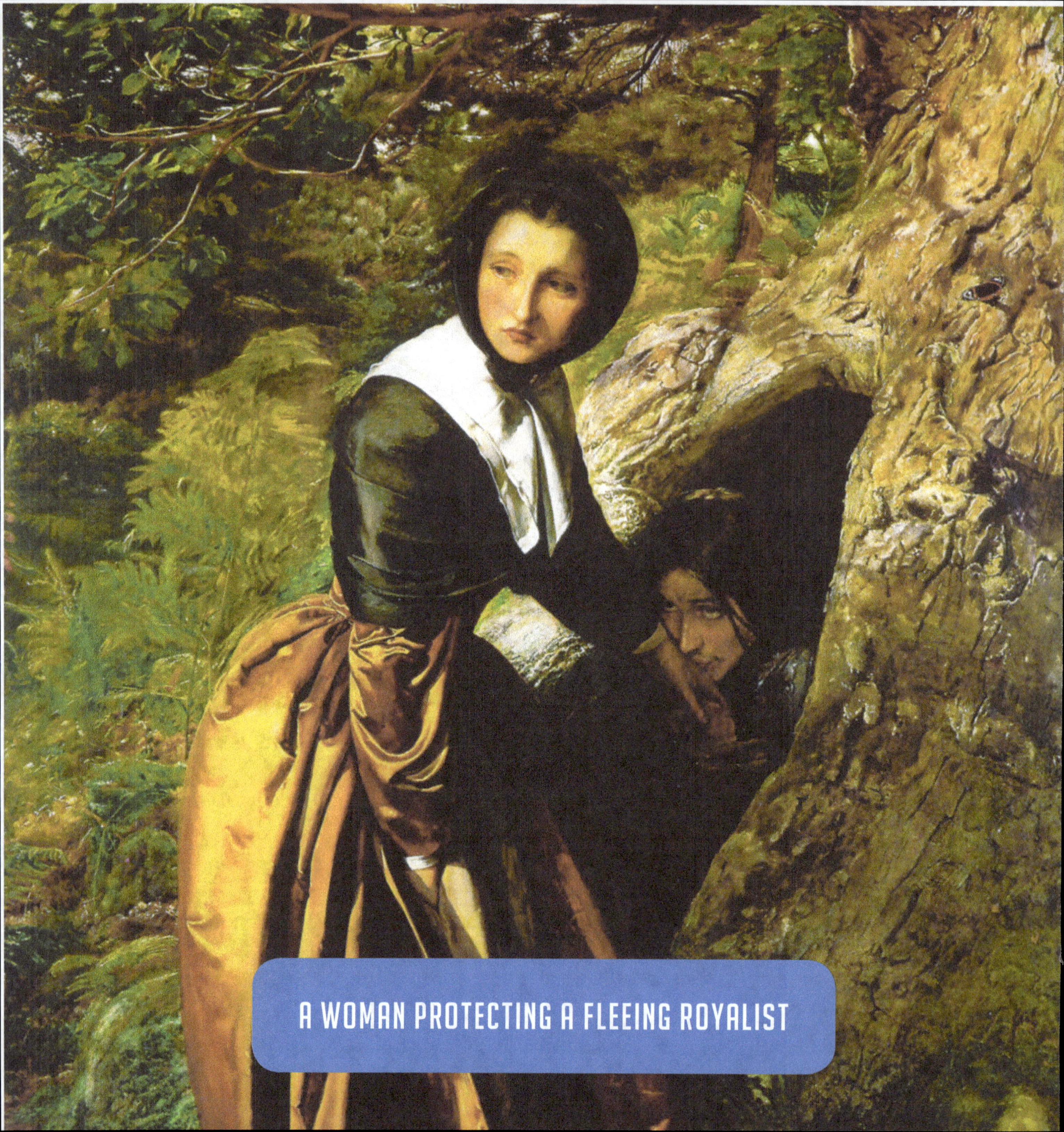
A WOMAN PROTECTING A FLEEING ROYALIST

FASCINATING FACTS ABOUT PATRIOTS AND LOYALISTS

Loyalists were also called Tories or Royalists. They were also known as King's Friends. Patriots were also called Whigs or Rebels. They were also known as Colonials.

Much of the fighting during the French and Indian War took place in the New York area, so many Loyalists were located there.

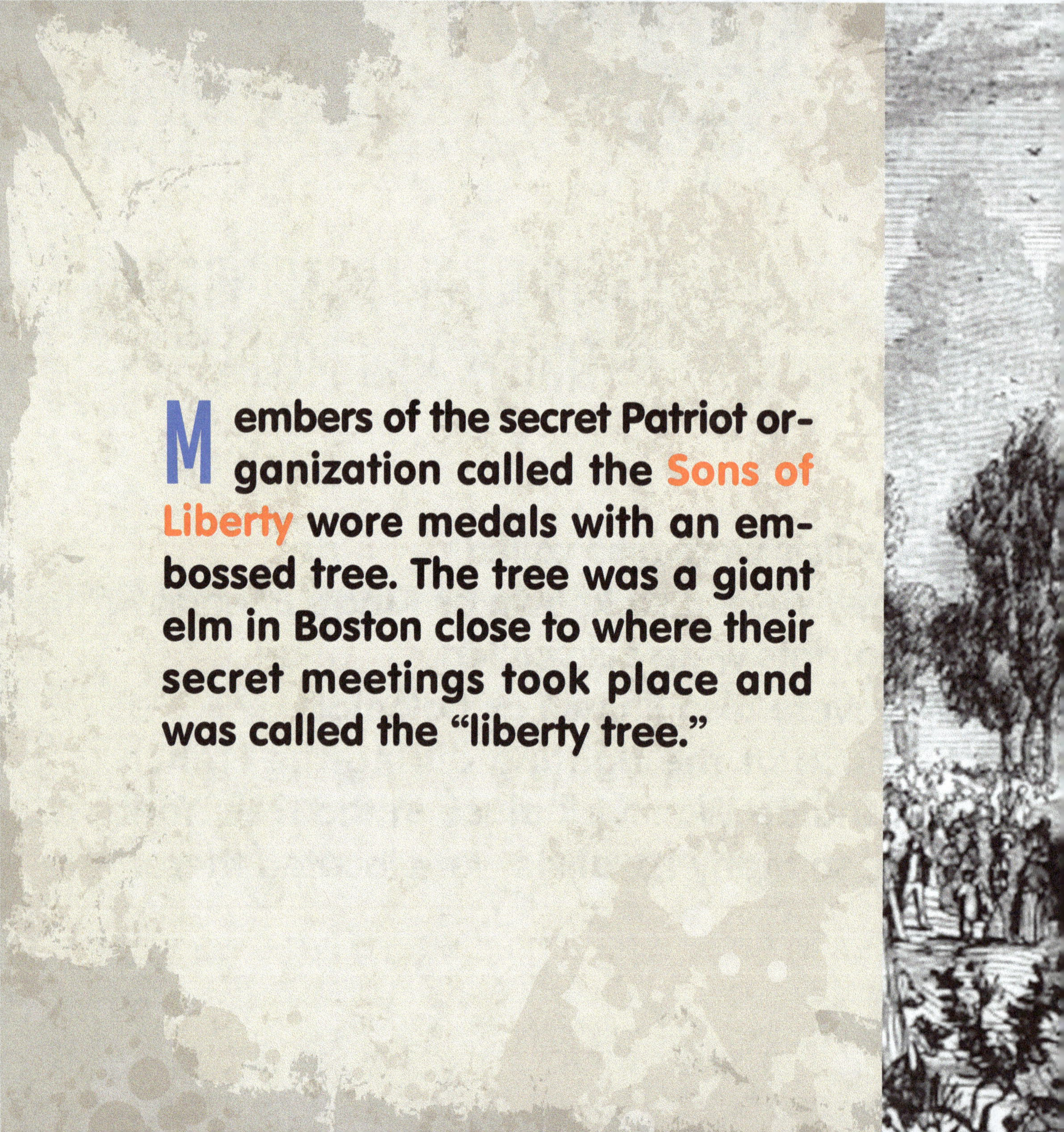

Members of the secret Patriot organization called the Sons of Liberty wore medals with an embossed tree. The tree was a giant elm in Boston close to where their secret meetings took place and was called the "liberty tree."

LIBERTY TREE IN BOSTON

FLAGS OF THE AMERICAN REVOLUTION

The Patriots had three types of committees that were essentially an acting government during the war: committees of correspondence, committees of safety, and committees of observation. In order to move about the country safely, citizens would have to swear that they were Patriots so they could be given passes to travel within lands that were controlled by Patriots.

Awesome! Now you know more about the history of the Loyalists and Patriots. You can find more American History books from Baby Professor by searching the website of your favorite book retailer.

Visit

BABY PROFESSOR
EDUCATION KIDS

www.BabyProfessorBooks.com
to download Free Baby Professor eBooks and view
our catalog of new and exciting Children's Books